For a Foot

Who Has it All

The Wonderful World of Football

Bruce Miller

ISBN 978-1-99-104862-2 (Paperback B&W)

ISBN 978-1-99-104863-9 (Paperback Color)

ISBN 978-1-99-104864-6 (Hardback B&W)

ISBN 978-1-99-104865-3 (Hardback Color)

Welcome to the wonderful world of football!

Football brings together young athletes, big money, and intense competition. Because of this, some incredible football/soccer stories have emerged that sound almost too exciting to be real.

And we have some doozies for you along with some that are rare and fascinating. The stories we've uncovered will surprise and delight every football fan.

Have you read about two referees who red-carded themselves during the game?

How about two teammates who got into a donnybrook causing the whole team to get into a brawl?

Or the goalkeeper who knocked himself out when he hit the side post during intense action on a foggy field?

You will find the answers on these pages, intriguing stories and facts your friends won't believe, plus football quizzes, and much more!

Stories of football history, amazing play and ability, and as years go by, more and more unique personalities are joining the fun and playing the beautiful game we all love.

Whether you call them quirky, unconventional or just plain crazy, their football stories will fascinate and put a smile on your face.

Get ready for an entertaining look at these amazing tales from the pitch, the grandstands, and the lives of those who play football!

1

That Awkward Moment When Your "Dead" Fan Shows Up to His Own Memorial. The Congleton HFS Loans League team was all set for a solemn moment of remembrance before their 1993 match. They planned to honor their oldest fan, who the PR team had been reliably informed died earlier that week.

But just as the minute of silent respect was set to begin, the crowd let out a collective gasp - because making his way through the gate was the "deceased" fan himself!

Turns out the old mate wasn't pushing up daisies after all. The club's PR folks might want to get their news from a source other than whoever said he graduated from this life and sent them down this embarrassing path.

They promptly canceled the memorial and dedicated that minute to watching their supposed departed fan enjoy the match instead. Some days it just doesn't pay to assume someone's gone on to that great stadium in the sky without double-checking!

When will England win the World Cup? Three elderly football fans hobble into a church, hoping for some

divine insight into their teams' fortunes and also to escape their nagging wives for a few hours.

The first, Larry "Scouse" Liverpool, pushes past the others and demands of the Big Guy upstairs, "Yo God, when's my squad gonna hoist the Premier League trophy again?"

The Man of Miracles checks his day planner and replies "A decade from now, mate. But it might be only my wishful thinking."

"Blimey," grumbles Larry, "at this rate the missus will have worn me out by then!"

Next up is old Artie "Spurs" Tottenham, who tries to knock Larry aside with his walker but ends up falling on his face. "Your Holiness," he croaks from the floor, "any idea when my boys will finally win some silverware?"

The Lord sighs heavily and says, "Twenty years from now, I'm afraid and watch your back - Larry's coming for your walker."

"Crickey," moans Artie, "at this rate the wife will have buried me under the porch by then!"

Finally, it's the turn of Three Lions Terry, still wearing his faded England jersey from 19966. Before he can ask his question, God booms in his best Cockney accent, "And what about you, mate - what's on your mind?"

Terry thinks a moment, then yells "Gov'nor! Last time When will the lads bring football home, eh?"

A heavenly chuckle echoes as the Almighty responds, "Sorry old boy, but at this rate even I'll be pushing up daisies and that's saying something! Now get out of here before your SWMBOs show up looking for you gents!"

No Limits to Learning! "I am not a perfectionist, but I like to feel that things are done well. Even more important than that, I feel an endless need to learn, to improve, to evolve, not only to please the coach and the fans, but also to feel totally satisfied with myself. It is my complete conviction that there are no limits to learning, and that it can never ever stop, no matter what our age."

-- Cristiano Ronaldo

Too Foggy. In 1937 on Boxing Day, Charlton faced off against Chelsea, and all seemed normal with the teams locked at 1-1. But suddenly, an ominous fog began to roll in, thickening rapidly across the pitch.

The referee paused the match, hoping the strange mist might soon clear. But instead of lifting, it only grew heavier. When play resumed, Bartram the goalkeeper stood tall in goal, keeping watch through the haze. "Our boys must have Chelsea on the ropes," he probably thought. But as Charlton attacked, fewer and fewer shapes could be seen.

Time passed in the strange fog, though no goals came. Still, the dutiful Bartram waited eagerly, certain his teammates were dominating. It was only when a lone figure emerged that the truth became clear. A puzzled policeman stared at the solitary keeper, asking, "Why are you still here? The match ended ages ago!"

Laughing teammates revealed Bartram had been left alone, unaware the game had been called due to zero visibility. It seems even the strangest of mists can play tricks on the mind. That day, one keeper found himself lost in a truly bizarre bank of Christmas fog!

A verse. *Twas the night before Christmas in 1937, on the foggy football field*

The Charlton keeper stood guard though the game had been sealed.

With pea soup for vision and no one in sight

He defended his net through the long winter night.

Twenty minutes he waited alone in the mist.

Till a bobby approached him and said "Son, you've persisted!"

"The match, it was canceled when fog rolled quite thick.

"But you stayed at your post, quite dedicated and kick.

Now come have some cocoa, your work here is done.

You defended with valor brave keeper, well done!"

Blind. In football, limiting one's perspective to only seeing the ball can be a detriment. As Brazilian playwright Nelson Rodrigues stated, "In football, a player is in fact blind if he only sees the ball." A well-rounded, strategic view considering all aspects of the game is most conducive to success.

Another foggy game. The lads at Arsenal decided to play a friendly game in pea soup fog against Dynamo Moscow back in 1945 at old White Hart Lane. Despite players begging the ref to call it on account of not being able to see their hand in front of their face, this ref insisted the show must go on.

6

The fog was thicker than a bowl of porridge. Both sides were making up rules as they went along, and no one had any idea of their own misfortune thanks to Old Man Winter playing a joke.

The Russkies at one point tried to pull a fast one by swapping players but not actually taking anyone off. The crowd swore they had 15 guys running around out there!

The Gunners made the most of it too - one lad they'd given his marching orders earlier snuck back on and finished the match without anyone noticing.

But it wasn't all fun and games - their keeper ran face-first into the goal post like a blind man sprinting through a screen door. Knocked himself clean out. With him in dreamland, a fan from the stands volunteered to man the sticks until he came to. Madness, I tell you!

Amazing Messi goal. Many fans have seen Messi score an incredible goal in the Barcelona vs. Getafe game which took place when Messi was only 19 years old.

It happened in April 2007, and it's amazing to watch if you happen to be one in sixteen million who haven't seen this on YouTube (the video is noted in the references in the back of this book). [1] The video which is in the references also has his humble explanation of how he did it and worth a watch. [2]

He has exceptional dribbling ability, and an almost psychic knowledge of advancing or passing the ball along with an almost magical and rare left foot.

Telling it like it is. "Without being too harsh on David Beckham, he cost us the match. My bad David, it's totally your fault we lost. Harsh enough?"

  -- Ian Wright. Television and radio personality and former professional footballer.

The Legend of The Dark Curse. While I do not believe in mystical hexes, the tale of Portuguese giants Benfica and their former boss Béla Guttmann is nothing short of astonishing. [3]

The great Guttmann led Benfica to back-to-back European Cup triumphs in 1961 and 1962. After the second straight title in '62, he approached club chiefs seeking a well-earned pay raise. Despite his unparalleled success, his request was denied.

As Guttmann stormed away from the club for the final time, he unleashed a chilling prophecy - "Not in a hundred years from now will Benfica ever be European champion again."

What followed can only be described as a curse of biblical proportions. Benfica went on to lose an unbelievable EIGHT straight European finals, including agonizing defeats in five European Cup showdowns in '63, '65, '68, '88 and '90. They also dropped three UEFA Cup/Europa League title tilts in '83, 2013 and 2014.

While Benfica was by far the stronger side in their 2013 and 2014 UEFA Cup championship matches against Chelsea and Sevilla, somehow victory continued to elude them, with the latter loss coming via a nail-biting penalty shootout.

Could the legend of a supposed curse place add mental pressure on Benfica's players and managers when it matters most, snatching triumph from the clutches of their talons yet again?

The curse might be lifted as in 2022, after losing three finals of the UEFA Youth League, Benfica's under-19 team finally became European youth champions by winning the 2021–22 edition. Time will tell.

That's happiness! "I'm as happy as I can be—but I have been happier. Like that one time I found a dollar on the sidewalk!"

-- Ugo Ehiogu. Ugo was a very successful player who not only won 2 Football League Cups with Aston Villa in 1996 but also added another with Middlesbrough in 2004! Ehiogu was an England international with an impressive record of 4 caps and 1 goal for the national team.

Can you believe in 1993 he became the first ever black player to captain England's under-21 team in a competitive match?

In 2012, Ugo briefly came out of retirement by signing with a non-league team called Wembley. He just wanted to play in some FA Cup games and hang out with other retired players. His desire was that he just wanted to have some fun competing one last time.

Unfortunately, he passed away way too young. He had a heart attack at Tottenham Hotspur's training facility at only 44 years old. His legacy and all he accomplished will definitely not be forgotten.

Ugo Ehiogu

A referee walks into a bar. Then into some chairs, then into a table, then straight into a post…

A strange but perhaps highly effective idea. This is a strange story. It's all about how to stop fans from running onto the pitch and causing disruptions.

There are a few ways to stop pitch invasions: electric fences, a heavy police presence, or making your team so bad that no fans turn up to run on the field in the first place. But the Romanian fourth division is a real wild west.

Back in 2003, Steaua Nicolae Balcescu had been threatened with expulsion from the league after a series of pitch invasions and fan fights.

The team certainly had a hooligan problem. Alex "Wildcard" Cringus thought of an unusual solution that hadn't been tried before to deal with it.

Now usually you'd think the chairman of a football team would have them playing in the top division, but these guys were stuck in the fourth tier. His solution? Fill a moat around the field with crocodiles! Can you believe that? A moat with man-eating crocs!

Cringus planned to get the scaley boys, throw them into a moat around the pitch and feed them meat from the local slaughterhouse. The ditch would be wide enough so that no one could jump across those hangry hissers. Anyone who tries will have to do the electric slide with the scaly pals! This will certainly stop fans from crashing the field once and for all.

This wasn't some half-baked scheme, though. Cringus had really thought this through. He planned to build the moat far enough back so the players wouldn't accidentally take a swan dive to their doom. He even considered the cold-bloodedness of the critters -- Romanian winters can be brutal so the water would be heated with electric pipes.

It would certainly fill stadium seats for the curious, but sadly, (no surprise) the local officials rejected it all.

Who Invented Football? The early forms of football arose independently in multiple ancient cultures and involved games that used hands more than kicking a ball. In ancient Greece, Phaininda and Episkyros were ball games played, with Episkyros being depicted on artwork from 375-400 BCE in Athens. Athenaeus described the Roman ball game of Harpastum from 228 CE. These games resembled rugby, wrestling and volleyball more than modern football due to the use of hands.

While football is now ubiquitous globally, the modern game is relatively young. Association football, also known as soccer, began with the first set of rules established by the Football Association in 1863 in England. Ebenezer Cobb Morley helped draft the original Laws of the Game that year. He certainly got a kick out of it (no pun intended).

Ebenezer Cobb Morely

One of the earliest recorded forms of football was "Cuju" played in China from 206 BC to 220 AD during the Han dynasty. Cuju literally translates to "kick ball" and involved kicking a ball into a net, prohibiting the use of hands like later English football.

The ancient Greek game of Episkyros also existed, involving two teams that could use their hands to pass a common ball. Episkyros and the related Roman game of Harpastum were often violent in nature.

The rules developed at the University of Cambridge in 1848, known as the Cambridge rules, had a significant influence on subsequent sets of rules for football games. This included the development of the rules for association football.

The organization now responsible for determining the Laws of the Game is the International Football Association Board. The International Football Association Board was formed in 1886 after representatives from FIFA and the four British football associations met in Manchester. FIFA, the international governing body of football, was established in 1904. At that time, FIFA agreed to adopt and follow the rules set by the Football Association.

For most of the 20th century, the countries of Europe and South America dominated international football competitions at the highest levels. Their national teams consistently achieved success when competing against other nations from around the world during this long period of the 1900s.

The FIFA World Cup beginning in 1930 showcased the strength of national teams. In the second half of the century, the European Cup and Copa Libertadores club competitions emerged, with their champions contesting the Intercontinental Cup.

Football as you know, is now played professionally worldwide, with billions watching games on television or online while millions still attend matches in person to support their favorite teams.

Bottles bearing names. At a heated local match between Arsenal and Tottenham last year, one fan found himself in the crossfire of a barrage of beer, cans, and more bottles.

"Relax kid, you've got nothing to fear," said the old-timer next to him...

"It's just like the bombs back in WWII. Unless a bottle has your name etched on it, it won't hit its target."

"That's precisely what's worrying me...", he replied to the supporter glumly, "my name is Johnny Walker."

Robbed of a draw. Time for some Danish fun now, and you have to feel bad for the poor lads from Ebeltoft FC who got robbed of a well-deserved draw against Norager in the local pub league.

Norager was ahead 4-3 with only seconds left on the clock when Ebeltoft said "one last hoorah!" and pushed forward for an equalizer.

But as they charged down the pitch, referee Henning "Gummy" Erikstrup blew his whistle - the only problem was, his choppers flew out of his mouth like a couple of dodgy dentures!

With old Gummy occupied picking his pearly whites off the pitch, Ebeltoft slotted one in to make it 4-all.

You'd think 4-4 was fair, but ol' Gummy wasn't having it. He waved off the goal and ended the match, handing Norager the win.

The Ebeltoft boys complained to the Danish dart boards association, but they wouldn't hear it. When the time is up, the time is up.

Final score: Norager 4, Ebeltoft 3. Tough luck, lads - better luck with the whistles next time!

Keep believing in yourself no matter your age.
As famous English goalkeeper Peter Shilton once said, "You've got to believe that you're going to win, and I believe we'll win the World Cup until the final whistle blows and we're knocked out. Then I'll believe we lost instead."

Peter Shilton was the goalkeeper for England at the FIFA World Cups in 1982, 1986, and 1990. In the 1986 World Cup, he famously faced Diego Maradona of Argentina who scored two goals against England, one being the controversial "Hand of God" goal.

Despite not making his debut in the World Cup finals until the age of 32, Shilton has played in 17 total World Cup final matches for England. He shares the record of 10 clean sheets in World Cup final matches with French goalkeeper Fabien Barthez. Shilton also represented England in the UEFA European Championships in 1980 and 1988 late in his career, showing that it's never too late to keep believing in yourself!

What was the highest scoring game in football history? Buckle up fans because this is a highly unusual story. The Madagascan football league, a competition you may not have heard much about but really should check out, was the site of an absolutely insane match.

AS Adema took on Stade Olympique de L'Emyrne and dominated in a way you cannot believe - they won 149-0 without scoring a single goal of their own!

We had to double check the score, but it's true. [4]

In a previous game earlier on in the tournament, SOE had a late penalty decision go against them, costing them a win. With their title hopes dashed, they decided to protest the call in the boldest way possible. It was a questionable penalty, and their disappointment was understandable and bad sportsmanship got the better of them.

In their next game, SOE players kicked the ball straight to their own goal over and over, with their keeper letting each one sail right in.

They booted in 149 shots into their own goals - can you imagine that many?! The crowd couldn't believe their eyes as SOE made one of the largest protest in sports history.

After the madness, league officials handed out suspensions to SOE's coach and some players. Both teams also received warnings.

This insane 149-0 result will forever stand out as one of football's strangest protests and biggest blowouts ever.

You have to respect the commitment to making a statement, even if scoring 149 own goals crossed a major line. This is one for the history books and the record still stands today! [5]

Normally football is a low scoring game, but there are two other strange high-scoring games. On July 7th, 2013, one of the craziest days in football history went down in Nigeria's lower leagues. Police Machine was taking on Bubayaro FC with a spot in the Nationwide League Division on the line. That's the bottom tier of pro ball over there.

Police Machine jumped out to a 6-0 lead in the first half. Then things totally unraveled for Bubayaro in the second. They started scoring own goals like crazy! By the end of the game, Bubayaro had somehow lost 67-0! You read that right. The Nigerian Football Federation was not happy either, calling it an "unacceptable" result and a "huge scandal."

In another game, Plateau United Founders destroyed Akurba 79-0! Akurba gave up 72 goals in the second half alone, many of them own goals. No surprise, but after looking into it, the head of competitions for the NFF banned all four teams for 10 years. Any players or refs involved got lifetime bans too. Crazy day for sure in the Nigerian leagues! [6]

Both high scoring games were the clubs chasing promotion and needing to boost their goal differences (scandalous scorelines).

Relatively speaking. "Alex Ferguson is the best manager I've ever had. In fact, he's the only manager I've actually had at this level. And he's the finest manager I've ever had. Not that I have much to compare him to..."

-- David Beckham.

Holding up the queue. Two old fans were holding up when the queue stopped right before the turn style trying to get into the stands before the game. One of them hunted for his ticket and was checking his coat pockets, waistcoat pockets and his trouser pockets, all to no avail...

"Hang on a minute...," said the gateman, "...what is that thing in your mouth?"

"It's the missing ticket!" gasped the old man scraping the ticket out.

As they moved inside his mate said..."What the hell, Cyril! It's sad to say but you might be getting senile in your old age. What's a ticket doing in your mouth and you forgetting about it!"

"Oh, 'I'm not that stupid. I was chewing last week's date off it."

Neymar's advice. Few know that Neymar gives sound advice to children by encouraging them to listen to and respect their parents. It's so important! He tells them that his father and mother have always been there giving him advice because they truly want the best for him. He tells all that he is very lucky to have their guidance and showing respect for your parents shows how much you appreciate all they do for you.

Do you remember these epic World Cup moments?! The FIFA World Cup is truly the greatest show on Earth! With the whole world on the edge of their seats for an entire month, the World Cup has provided countless unforgettable scenes, some so hilarious that they still make fans laugh out loud today!

Jimmy Greaves' canine catch was comedic gold during the legendary 1962 quarterfinal between England and Brazil. The Chelsea and Spurs great stole the show by hilariously leaping to scoop up a stray pup - one of the most amusing moments in World Cup history for sure!

Alejandro Sabella's awkward stumble in 2014 was priceless too. As Argentina faced Belgium in the quarters, the late coach almost took a tumble before being saved by his staff. Even the highest stakes games can produce hilarious mishaps!

Graham Poll's epic refereeing blunder in 2006. Graham allowed Croatian Josip Simunic to stay in the match after two yellow cards against Australia, only sending him off after a third?! Even the officials aren't immune to memorable mistakes.

Rivaldo's dramatic dive in 2002 also had us in stitches. When the Turkish player kicked the ball to him for a corner and it hit his leg, the Brazilian great pretended it smacked him in the face instead! The ref fell for it, giving Turkey a red card. Rivaldo's acting skills are truly world class. Check it out on YouTube in the references. [7]

The 1990 incident between Rudi Völler and Frank Rijkaard gave us an unexpected laugh as well. When the Dutchman spat in Völler's hair after a booking. They later made up and posed together in an ad. Just goes to show, even the most heated rivalries produce priceless moments!

Fall down. How could we forget Thomas Muller's bizarre, failed attempt at a sneaky free kick in 2014? For the first 90 minutes of Germany's round of 16 match against Algeria, it was like their bodies had been possessed by the ghosts of the drunken spectators from the stands above.

Goalkeeper Manuel Neuer repeatedly sprinted out of his area as if his shorts were filled with fire ants and even leading goal scorer Thomas Muller suddenly seemed to have the hand-eye coordination of Stevie Wonder trying to thread a needle.

This bizarre phenomenon reached its comedic peak late in regular time when Germany attempted to execute the most elaborate free-kick routine since the Munich circus came to town, but Muller fell down on his run-up like a newborn foal.

It was unclear if the stumble was intentional or if Muller's legs had simply forgotten how to kick a ball, but either way the free kick crashed and burned harder than Lindsay Lohan's career. Needless to say, the Algerians were rolling.

But just as it looked like Germany would be launching an "Investigation Discovery" episode about themselves, the magic (or lack thereof) vanished from their bodies as quickly as it had come, and Andre Schurrle tapped in a beauty to break the hex. Sanity, as well as the scoreline, had been restored.

The World Cup seems to always finds creative new ways to entertain us!

Thomas Muller

Some things you can't change. "In his life, a man can
change wives, political parties or religions but he cannot change his favourite football team."

-- **Eduardo Galeano**, a prominent Uruguayan journalist, writer, and novelist. He is regarded by many as a major figure in Latin American left-wing literature. In addition, Galeano is viewed as one of the foremost writers on the global sport of football.

Quiz question 1. When taking a free kick in football, a player is permitted to lift the ball with either one foot or both feet simultaneously in order to kick it. The player is not required to use only one foot when executing a free kick.

True or false?

Answer on p. 98

Say what? "I would not be bothered if we lost every game as long as we won the league. And got a participation trophy!"

-- **Mark Viduka** is an Australian football player who played as a center forward. He captained Australia at the 2006 World Cup, which is still their joint-best performance ever at that tournament. And get this - his four goals in the Champions League are still more than any other Australian to score in that competition. To this day he still holds the record.

A keeper. Why do most women avoid dating a football player?

A. If they are planning to settle down, they don't date a player since there's only a 1/11 chance, they are a keeper.

Horsing around. Ol' Ned the Donkey was feeling pretty thirsty one afternoon, so he walked on over to his pal, Horace the Horse, for a cold one.

When Ned walked in, he about fell over in shock - Horace's walls were covered in more bling than a Kardashian Christmas party.

"Good gravy Horace, did you rob a trophy store?" Ned exclaimed.

Horace whinnied with pride. "Back in my day I was quite the racehorse - won more ribbons than a box of Cracker Jack. You're looking at the Kentucky Derby champ three years running!"

Ned was duly impressed.

After a few more drinks, they decided Ned's bachelor pad was next on the party circuit. But Ned started sweating - his walls were emptier than Eeyore's birthday card. He had to come up with something fast!

The next day, Ned sneaked into the city zoo and snapped a photo of a particularly handsome zebra. He framed the picture and hung it proudly.

When Horace showed up that week, Ned played it cool. "Like my new artwork?" he asked casually.

Horace squinted suspiciously. "Ned...is that you? I thought you used to play striker for Inter Milan!"

Ned replied, "No that's when Rinaldo asked me to play for Juventus!" and winked and poured them each another beverage.

The Story of Young Mauricio, Bolivia's First Wonder Boy of Football. This is a story about the youngest person to ever play professionally.

On July 19, 2009, a marvelous event took place in the lands of Bolivia. In the city of La Paz, during a match between the clubs of Aurora and the locals, a last-minute substitution was made that would entrance all those witnessing.

For on that day, young Mauricio Baldivieso, just shy of his thirteenth year, took to the field playing for Aurora. At only twelve seasons in age, he had become the youngest in all of Bolivia to ever play the gentleman's game at a level of the professionals.

Word of the feat of young Mauricio spread far and wide across the plains and mountains of Bolivia. All wondered at this boy's talents and precocity to be allowed to join the men in competition. It was revealed that his father, Julio Baldivieso, the manager of Aurora, had made the choice to send his son out to experience the game. And amazingly his father's decision was a good one since Mauricio did not disappoint, showing poise and skill well beyond what would be expected of one so young.

Two years later in 2011, fate would see father and son reunited at Aurora once more. With Julio taking the managerial role for a second time, Mauricio also returned to the club. Playing under his father's guidance, the young star saw increased playing time, making nineteen appearances in the league and even finding the net three times with his boot!

Bolivia had found itself a wunderkind and prodigy of football, this Mauricio Baldivieso. As of today, Mauricio is the youngest person ever to play professional football. [8]

Remember "The Game of the Century?" This was a 1970 FIFA World Cup semifinal between Italy and West Germany has been dubbed "The Game of the Century." Many say the match had it all! [9]

It was played on June 17th, 1970, at the legendary Estadio Azteca in Mexico City. Italy emerged victorious 4-3 in the highest scoring *overtime game* in World Cup history, eliminating Germany from the tournament as they went on to lose to Brazil in an equally epic final.

Italy jumped out to an early lead thanks to Roberto Boninsegna's goal in the 8th minute. Then fast forward to the 70th minute, German star Franz Beckenbauer played on despite a dislocated shoulder, what guts!

Late in regular time, defender Karl-Heinz Schnellinger shocked everyone by equalizing for Germany in the 90th minute. And, after 90 minutes of nail-biting action, the teams were deadlocked at 1-1.

Then overtime brought even more almost incredible drama! Gerd Müller put Germany ahead early in overtime, but Tarcisio Burgnich tied it right back up shortly thereafter! Italian legend Gigi Riva then scored a magnificent goal to put Italy back on top. But could they hold on?!

Gerd Müller wasn't done, scoring another diving header to make it 3-3.

But with the replay of that goal still going, Gianni Rivera scored the biggest goal of his life in the 111th minute off a perfect assist from Boninsegna.

Italy had done it, winning an instant classic 4-3 in one of the greatest games in the beautiful game's rich history! [10]

The longest football marathon and the longest match. According to the Guinness Book of World Records, the *longest marathon* playing football is 168 hours, and was achieved by SF Winterbach and TGIF-EC Wallhalben (Both DE), in Winterbach, Germany, from 29 May to 5 June 2019.

The final score was SF Winterbach 1,797 - TGIF-EC Wallhalben 1,830. Over 30 Referees officiated the match. [11]

The longest *match* game ever took place way back in 1946. Stockport County faced off against Doncaster Rovers at Edgeley Park on March 30th, and this game just did not want to end!

It started as a Division Three North Cup replay after their first game ended in a 2-2 tie. Well, this one went into extra time all tied up at 2-2 again after 90 minutes.

They played another 30 minutes but still no one could score. Can you believe they played for over 3 hours and 23 minutes total! Stockport even thought they had scored the winner in the 173rd minute but it got called back.

It was getting too dark to see by that point since there weren't lights in most fields back then. So, they had to call it after over 203 minutes of play without a winner.

Simple rules. "The rules of football are very simple, basically it is this: if it moves, kick it. If it doesn't move, kick it until it does."

— **Phil Woosnam**. As a player, he played for five clubs in England and one club in the United States. He represented Wales at the international level in football. Woosnam was described as a gifted inside-forward, who also demonstrated high football intelligence on the field.

After his playing career, Woosnam served as the commissioner of the North American Football League from 1969 to 1982. In this role, he oversaw the expansion and growth period of the league. Under his leadership as commissioner, the NASL grew substantially both in the number of teams and the popularity of professional football (soccer) in North America.

In recognition of his contributions to soccer in the United States both as a player and administrator, Woosnam was inducted into the U.S. National Soccer Hall of Fame in 1997. The Hall of Fame honors those individuals who have made important contributions to the sport in the United States.

Phil Woosnam 1975

Rule question thinking out of the box. This might sound a bit insane, but is it against the rules if you were somehow able to bite into the ball and carry it in for a goal? It is a bit hard to imagine anyone doing that. Theoretically yes, it seems legal since the only part of your body you can't touch the ball with is your arm from shoulder down.

Players have balanced the ball behind their neck and walk with the ball on their neck but not very fast. It's easy to knock the ball off by heading it or nudging their body to make the ball fall. Shoving or charging is banned, but standing next to someone and giving a shoulder or torso nudge isn't. But fans dislike that since it doesn't help the team and may even be stopped by the ref as unsportsmanlike behavior.

But let's assume for a second that someone had jaws of steel and could totally sink their teeth into the ball without using their hands. The football is roughly 22 cm (8.66 inches) in diameter for a regulation size 5 ball. Rules state that a size 5 ball must be 68 to 70 cm (27 to 28 inches) in circumference.

If someone could actually grip the ball in their mouth without handling it first, some argue the ref would have to call an indirect free kick since biting the ball is just too wild and puts other players at risk if they try to challenge for it. No one wants a face full of teeth!

So as tricky as it would be, mouth-carrying the ball probably counts as playing dangerously. What's your opinion?

Not slaves! "Some people tell me that we professional players are football slaves. Well, if this is slavery, give me a life sentence."

-- **Bobby Charlton.** Widely considered one of the greatest players of all time, he was a member of the England team that won the 1966 FIFA World Cup, the year he also won the Ballon d'Or.

Some thoughts on high kicks. In the recent Women's World Cup, there were some high jinks and funny incidents involving the rules for high kicks.

First, in a game between Australia and Nigeria, there was an incident around the second Nigerian goal. The attacker went for a header on a ball at head height. The defender went for a high side kick-type clearance. You'll never guess what happened next - the attacker cleanly won the race and scored!

But get this - the defender kicked the attacker so hard in the chest that she spent several minutes being treated by the medical team. Ladies, ladies!

It was very unusual though that after the goal was awarded there no cards at all! Can you believe there was no yellow, and they didn't even flash out a red?

Second, in a game between China and Haiti, there was again, a ball at head height. The Chinese defender goes for and cleanly wins the header. But the attacker decides to go for the overhead kick anyway! The only problem is, she misses the ball completely and kicks the defender square in the kisser!

She only got a yellow card slap on the wrist for almost taking the poor girl's head off! In most people's views that red card should have been out faster than you can say "off with her foot!" But I guess nearly decapitating someone with your boot is just considered "just a little bit reckless" in ladies' footy.

As far as most are concerned, if you're swinging those size nines around people's noodles, you'd better be darn sure you not going to clonk anyone. But it seems like the refs aren't handing out cards for head shots despite Law 12 prohibiting "playing dangerously."

The Heavenly Kingdom v. The Underworld.
Shortly after the apocalypse wrapped up, an issue arose regarding' the border between the pearly gates and the fiery pit.

God called up ole Beelzebub for a chinwag to sort this dustup quick.

Satan, the big red guy himself, suggested they settle it with some football.

The good Lord chuckled and said to Lucifer "That smoke must have fried your brains, it'd be no contest at all! All the best players head up top, ya know."

The devil just grinned and replied "Sure, sure, but we got all the refs in our back pocket..."

Confidence. "If you don't believe you can win, there is no point in getting out of bed at the end of the day. Might as well sleep in and miss the whole game!"

-- Neville Southall, a Welsh former international footballer. He has been described as one of the best goalkeepers of his generation and won the FWA Footballer of the Year award in 1985.

Neville Southall, 2007

Referees Gone Rogue. First a story about Andy Wain, the referee who whistled himself off the pitch.

The referee's job isn't easy - they have to wrangle with 22 players and keep their cool under pressure. But Andy gave himself his own red card!

This happened during a classic Sunday pub league grudge match between the Postal Workers and the Village Idiots. Things were getting chippy as the lads worked up a thirst.

When Village Idiots' keeper Ricky complained that Andy missed an obvious trip in the box, the ref saw red!

He whipped off his whistle, got in Ricky's face and looked about two seconds from dropping the gloves. Luckily for all involved, no fisticuffs ensued.

But Andy Wain must have realized he lost his marbles, so he brandished the rare self-red and ended the match early. The lads all went to the pub to settle it over pints, because that's what Sunday league is all about!

It was reported Andy felt he shouldn't have officiated as he was going through various personal problems for several days before the match. He felt his conduct and anger was indeed unprofessional and if a someone on the pitch did the same, he'd red card them. But fortunately, he quickly came to his senses.

The second instance of self-red carding happened with referee Melvin Sylvester, who went one step further, by physically attacking a player during a fixture between Southampton Arms and Hurstbourne Tarrant British Legion in the Andover and District Sunday League.

"I was sorely provoked," explained Sylvester afterwards. "I punched him several times after he had pushed me from behind. He then swore. I couldn't take it anymore. I blew my top."

They kept playing after what happened. One of the fans ended up taking over as referee for the rest of the match. But Sylvester's story didn't end there. After that, the local football association fined him 20 GBP and suspended him for six weeks. I guess they didn't appreciate him walking off the field like that during the game.

Precision. "Playing football is like making a watch. You need natural talent, and any elegance means nothing without discipline, rigour, and precision."

-- Lionel Messi

Lionel Messi

Balotelli stories. Some have the opinion that Mario Balotelli is without a doubt the Mayor of Madnessville. He's the Duke of Daffyness, the Earl of Erratic Behavior, and his sense of humour is over the top unique.

He made a name for himself by coupling his amazing talent with mad-hatter antics, and holds a special place in the hearts of football fans around the globe. In his day, Balotelli was absolutely fabulous thanks to his brand of swashbuckling bravado and unrelenting self-confidence.

Sadly, despite being one of the most talented players of his generation, Balotelli's player career in most opinions only ever simmered, never reaching the violent boil that many had expected. That may be due to his ne'er-do-well attitude that blighted his career as he lurched from one controversy to the next.

Here are just a few stories of Mario's madcap misadventures over the years.

- First, some say young Mario started his crazy antics with his urinating nonsense at Lumezanne, where he was known to relieve himself on people's luggage, fresh laundry, and sometimes even the lads themselves! Talk about marking your territory!

- Team spirit usually demands that one not show support for rivals. Nevertheless, he openly supporting AC Milan while playing for Inter Milan. He enjoyed some success after signing for Inter but after showing his love for fierce rivals AC Milan in interviews that was never gonna fly.

- On another occasion he ignored Jose Mourinho's plea not to get a red card. As Inter Milan's sole striker in an important Euro match, Jose begged the already-carded Mario to cool it. But just 9 minutes into the second half, Balotelli was seeing red. Some things are hard to change!

- Mario went shopping for an ironing board for his new Man City pad, and came back with a quadbike, trampoline and Scalextric set. I think it's safe to say the City bosses knew they were in for a wild ride!

- How many players do you know of who were fined £100k for lobbing darts at the City academy kids from a first-floor window? Why did he do this? He simply said, "I was bored."

- Running clean through on goal, he tried to showboat with an outrageous backheel finish. Of course, he fluffed it and was immediately taken off by an irate Roberto Mancini.

- Fireworks in the bathroom. Who else do you might know who did thousands in damage by setting off fireworks indoors. The next day he wore his famous "Why always me?" shirt before, ironically, becoming the face of firework safety. Only Mario!

After leaving City, Mario bounced around clubs like Marseille and Monza. He was filmed giving a teammate a few one-two punches after being subbed off in Turkey. Who else hits their own teammate who hasn't done anything to you?

Mario seems to have done so many unusual things both on and off the pitch that he truly puts the "fun" in dysfunction. Driving onto campuses without permission to use the can? Classic Mario! Bonkers yet strangely entertaining.

It's tough to say what's really going on in that mad hatter brain of his. But one thing is for sure - he is without a doubt the most untamed footballer in the game.

Mario as well as most everyone doesn't like racism. He's been quoted as saying,

"You know, racist people are really in the minority these days. But there's not much you can do to change them, you know?

Like you can talk to them and do whatever, but it probably won't make a difference cause they're just stubborn like that. When I was coming up, I had tons of friends and almost all of them were Italian. It's weird cause the racism really only started when I started playing football professionally."

Mario, like many players in the public's eye has said,

"The way people see me in the media is totally not an accurate picture of who I am as a person. What matters most is that the people who actually know me understand what I'm really like. Folks who don't know me personally just read the papers and watch TV. And TV is all about opinions, you know? So, I can't show everyone the real me."

He knows he's unique. *"I'm super proud to be Italian because that's where I was born and raised, went to school, and made my career. I'm Italian through and through. And honestly, you'd be hard pressed to find anyone else quite like me! If you do, dinner is on me!"*

Say again? Question: "Barry, how did you prepare for a game when you were a player?"

A. "Well, I put my right boot on first, and I did that all the time. Then, of course, I put on my right sock. Wait…left sock? I ah… What did I say?"

    -- **Barry Venison.** Former English football coach and professional footballer. After he retired, he was a television pundit and was very well known on ITV Sport's "The Premiership" show between 2001 and 2004 while the network had the right to show Premier League highlights.

Later on in 2016, he got a head coach position for the first time with the Orange County Blues, succeeding the coach, Oliver Wyss.

Challenging the referee. The loosing head coach, always one to question a call, sidled up to the ref and said, "Wow! What a game that was, am I right?!"

"You think so, eh?" grinned the ref, eating it up.

"You betcha!" replied the coach. "Too bad you were too busy looking at your phone and scrubbing' the dirt off your glasses to catch any of the action!"

Yeah right! "I couldn't settle in Italy—it was like living in a foreign country. They spoke some weird language called 'Italian' or something."

-- **Ian James Rush.** He is regarded as one of the best strikers of all time and one of the best Welsh players in the history of the sport. Then he played for Liverpool (1980–1996 approximately) where he was and still is the club's all-time leading goal scorer. His record there is a total of 346 goals for club competitions.

Confusing. "I have to think about this one. We lost because we didn't win. Or maybe it was because the other team scored more goals than us?"

-- **Ronaldo.**

Blaming. Three hapless homers were commiserating over their hometown team's hapless play.

The first fan blamed...: "If you ask me, it's all that manager's fault. I mean, what does he know? We'd be lifting trophies left and right if he'd just sign some studs already."

The second fan blamed...: "Pssh, it ain't the manager's fault. Our guys are clearly just dogging it out there. Maybe if they pulled their heads out and hustled for once we'd score more than a field goal a game."

The third fan blamed...: "You guys are both wrong. This is clearly Mom and Dad's doing. If they had just popped me out in this town, I'd be cheering for a real contender!"

Recruitment of the mythical Bulgarian Striker

"Tittyshev" During a friendly match between West Ham and Oxford United, manager Harry Redknapp was having a bit of trouble. Not only were his boys getting trounced on the pitch, but one loud-mouthed fan in particular - a tattooed gent called Steve Davies - was ruthlessly heckling from the stands.

With injuries mounting and subs exhausted, cunning Harry spotted an opportunity. "Oi Steve!" he called, "Fancy showing us how it's done since you seem to know better?"

Much to Redknapp's delight, Steve reluctantly agreed to lace up his boots. Lo and behold, the man scored within minutes of entering the game!

As the stadium announcer prepared to identify West Ham's new secret weapon, a sly smile spread across Harry's face. "Just tell them it's the one and only Bulgarian striker Tittyshev," he chuckled. And that, kids, is how West Ham unearthed the legendary "Tittyshev" and shut up one mouthy fan for good. All's well that ends well, as they say!

The largest stadium in the world. According to the

Guinness Book of World Records, as of March 2014, the largest football venue by capacity is the Rungnado May Day Stadium (aka the 1st of May Stadium) in Pyongyang, North Korea, with a current capacity of 150,000. It was built after South Korea hosted the 1988 Summer Olympics.

Following the Summer Olympics in South Korea, the stadium began operation in 1989. The playing space in the center of the stadium is 22,500 m². It is eight stories high with seats going up to that level and has 16 arch shaped petal-like sections.

Rungnado May Day Stadium in Pyongyang, North Korea

Ibrahimovic – "The Humbleness Jersey." Here's one story old by the legendary Zlatan. Towards the end of Ibrahimovic's career, he decided to go to LA Galaxy.

In his statement, he said: "I decided to sign with Galaxy because I think it's the right place for me."

Most any regular player would say that and get back to training. Instead, Zlatan took out a full-page advert in the LA Times announcing his arrival at LA Galaxy.

That's the end, right? No. LeBron James, already playing for the Lakers, sends his jersey to Zlatan to welcome him to LA. Zlatan signed it and mailed it back to LeBron.

Zlatan Ibrahimovic

Quiz question 2. Which of the following pitches would not be allowable under IFAB laws?

A. A field 100 yards long and 95 yards wide

B. A field 130 yards long and 50 yards wide

C. A field with artificial turf

D. A field painted blue

Answer on p. 98

Stuck. "I've never wanted to leave, and I plan to be here until I pass away, and perhaps even after that too. You are simply stuck with me forever!"

-- **Alan Shearer.** Alan was chosen by the Football Writers' Association as the player of the year in 1994. Also adding to his honors, he won the PFA Player of the Year award in 1995. His awards continued and the next year, he came third in both Ballon d'Or and FIFA World Player of the Year awards.

Later on in 2004, he was chosen by Pelé in the FIFA 100 list of the world's greatest living players and in 2021 he was inducted into the Premier League Hall of Fame.

Cristiano Ronaldo -- The Relentless Competitor. Ronaldo's intensely competitive nature has long been evident. Scouts recognized this drive when assessing his talent and mentality during his origins in Portugal.

Former teammate Patris Evra recounted a telling anecdote from their Manchester United days. During a table tennis match, Rio Ferdinand defeated Ronaldo, much to Evra and others' delight.

However, Ronaldo refused to accept defeat. He resolutely ordered a table tennis table for home practice. For two weeks straight, he honed his skills to become superior.

Upon returning, Ronaldo challenged Ferdinand and emerged victorious in front of the team, proving his resolve. As Evra noted, this unflinching competitiveness fuels Ronaldo's desire to again win Player of the Year and lift the World Cup trophy with Portugal. He is a man on a singularly determined mission for success.

Christiano Rinaldo

The Little Magician Strikes Again. The debate continues to rage on - is Messi or Rinaldo the greatest of all time? The GOAT arguments are endless about both of these amazing players. But witnessing Messi's magic in person is something else entirely.

As the story goes, during a fierce El Clasico clash, Messi's side momentarily lost possession. Instead of dropping back as most would, the Argentine maestro boldly demanded the ball from his keeper. Without a moment's hesitation, the goalie rolled him the leather. What happened next can only be described as the stuff of legend.

The Little Magician embarked on a scintillating solo run, dancing past defenders once considered the finest in the business. Through the likes of Yaya Toure, Puyol, Iniesta and Xavi he slalomed, as if they weren't even there. When he reached the danger area, the ball was placed with pinpoint precision into the back of the net.

For Messi to do it against "some of the best in the world," not just once but multiple times, was otherworldly. Even Zidane and Ronaldinho in their pomp didn't seem to attempt the audacious.

Fans feel Messi is a player who had transcended the boundaries of what was possible on a football pitch. The legend of Messi had been forged.

But Messi only considers himself a humble team player. *"I like and enjoy winning titles with the team more than I do for individual awards or scoring more goals than anyone else. My main concern is being a good person than being the best in the world. When all this is over, what do you have? What's left? When I retire, I hope I am remembered for being a noble, reasonable and decent man."* - Lionel Messi

The clock. All true Red Devils know why 3:30 lives forever in their hearts. On February 6th, 1958, the United squad were soaring home from Belgrade, victorious after battle against the Warriors of Red Star. Little did they suspect that fate had other plans, and that most would never see Old Trafford again.

Pilots James and Kenneth twice aborted takeoff as their starboard engine surged and sputtered. Yet Captain Thain seemed to refuse to surrender to the night, and determined to defeat the gathering darkness.

Snow now swirled as the plane raced down the runway, and their wings met a wall of white slush hiding at the end. The left wing tore away as the brave bird struck the fence, and Manchester United fell into disaster.

But their spirit could not be broken. Though Sir Matt suffered wounds that might have slain lesser men, he vowed to rebuild what was lost.

Step by step they climbed, winning the Cup in '63 and the crown in '65 and '67. But the boss demanded more - the boss would settle for nothing less than European glory.

And so, in 1968 at Wembley before all of England, United conquered the Kings of Lisbon, Benfica, 4-1. Two who survived that darkest of days, Foulkes and captain Charlton, found redemption in victory. Ten years after tragedy, the Red Devils had completed their rise and claimed their rightful place among the legends of world football.

The clock that struck 3:30 would remind them forever of the price of dreams, and of the triumph of an unbreakable human will.

Fast question. What did the bad football announcer get for Christmas?

COOOOOOOOOOAAAAAAAAAAAAAAAAAAAAAAAAAA ALLLLLLLLLLLLLLLLLLLLLL!!!!!!!!!!!!!!!!!!!!!!

Didn't ever back down. Diego Maradona was one of the most unique and colorful personalities in the history of football, but that uniqueness partly contributed to his incredible skills on the field.

He was always willing to stand up to opponents much larger than himself, as evidenced by his willingness to engage in confrontations. Maradona never backed down from a fight.

Maradona lived life to its fullest. He immersed himself in the diverse communities where he played the game, developing connections with different groups of people. While some of his personal choices were controversial, he approached each new experience with courage and determination.

When faced with unwarranted intrusions on his privacy, Maradona's response, though ill-advised, took pot shots at the reporters out of frustration with the constant hounding by the press.

Lots of talent from everywhere. "Germany are a very difficult team to play...they had 11 internationals out there today."

-- **Steve Lomas**, Northern Irish football manager and former professional footballer.

Unusual World Cup Final Games.

The year 1930. The nations of Argentina and Uruguay had agreed before the tournament began that they would play their matches with their own preferred balls. Yet as fortune would have it, these two rivals found themselves facing each other in the final match.

Belgian referee John Langenus, who officiated the game dressed in a fine shirt, tie, blazer and knickerbockers, supposedly said, "The deep animosity between the two countries was exposed when the time came to decide on a ball, both teams fiercely demanded to play with their own ball."

FIFA president Jules Rimet was forced to make a ruling, decreeing that they would use each nation's ball for half the game. And it did indeed make a difference. Argentina, using a ball imported from the fine country of Scotland, took a two-goal lead by the halftime break.

Yet Uruguay, with a ball bought in England, fought back in the second half. And it was Hector Castro, known by his countrymen as 'El Manco' for having lost his arm in an accident long ago, who secured the victory for Uruguay with a score of four to two.

The year 1950. On the very day of the decisive match held inside the great temple recently built to host such an event, the Brazilian newspaper O Mundo ran a photo of their national team on its front page alongside a headline proclaiming "Here Are The World Champions."

Captain Obdulio Varela of Uruguay was enraged upon seeing this. He purchased twenty copies of the paper, scattered them across the floor of the hotel toilet, and chalked upon the mirrors "Trample and urinate on these newspapers." Varela then commanded his teammates to visit the lavatory and carry out his instructions.

Brazil needed only a draw to take the title, and indeed led one-nil at the half.

But those fiery Uruguayans, spurred on by their roaring leader, came from behind to win two-goals-to-one and lift the trophy.

On that day, the Uruguayans had disgraced Brazilian newspapers and dreams both in the toilet and upon the field.

The year 1954. Herbert Zimmerman had accepted his duty - to describe to millions listening on German radio each Hungarian goal as it came.

The Magical Magyars had earlier trounced Deutschland eight-goals-to-three and held a record thirty matches unbeaten.

Within eight minutes Zimmerman had called two Hungarian scores. Later he said, "I wished only to limit how many more we would concede." Yet West Germany battled back to equalize, and in the eighty-fourth minute the ball found the feet of Helmut Rahn.

"Rahn shoots! Goal! Goal! Goal! Goal!" cried Zimmerman, before falling deathly silent as the import of the moment took him.

After eight seconds, just as listeners feared their wireless had failed, Zimmerman regained himself and bellowed in triumph "Goal for Germany! Germany led three-goals-to-two. Call me mad, call me crazy!"

The publications Kicker, La Gazzetta dello Sport and The Guardian all agreed this was one of the most iconic piece of football commentary in history.

The year 1970. Incredibly, Tostao played the last twenty minutes against Italy through relentless and grateful tears. The balletic playmaker, now playing in an unfamiliar striker role, had suffered a detached retina on the cusp of the tournament and was told his career was at its end.

So, it turned out - at just twenty-six years of age and closely following emergency surgery in Houston, Texas and encouragement from Pele, manager Mario Zagallo included him. Tostao was a left-footed forward.

"After the third goal, the one securing our victory, I was overwhelmed by emotion," Tostao recounted to FIFA, "I began crying and could not stop. I thought of all I endured to play in this World Cup, how close I came to missing out.

I traveled the world for surgery on my eye and almost wasn't allowed to join the team. It was truly difficult to play again.

When I knew we would be champions, I couldn't hold back my tears."

He left the pitch in just his undergarments even though they tried to remove those too.

He did have his World Cup winner's medal, which he gave to the ophthalmologist who performed surgery on his eye.

Tostao

The year 1986. Disaster struck Don José Luis Brown of Argentina, who had tossed the mighty Diego Maradona of Germany to the turf to head home the opening goal against the Germans in the finale, when he did dislocate his shoulder just after the midday sun. The game was surely at its end. Or so we all thought.

"The pain was beyond bearing," explained Brown, "but I told the sawbones in no uncertain terms, 'Think not of removing me from the field.' I bit a hole in my jersey, and did place my finger through it to fashion a sling,"

Brown was removed from the battlefield for only 28 seconds and did fight on for the remainder of the contest as Argentina did defeat the Germans 3 goals to 2.

By the way Andreas Brehme of Germany scored goals with both his right and left feet in this grand tournament.

José Luis Brown

The year 1990. Lothar Matthaus of Germany did calmly strike home the lone goal from the spot against the Czechs in the quarterfinals. Yet when awarded another penalty with but 5 minutes remaining in the final hour, 85 minutes into a contest with no goals, Andreas Brehme did curiously elect to take the shot.

"I cracked the sole of my boot in the first half," explained Matthaus. "I had no other to wear, so I made do with the lone spare the kitman had. They did not fit as they should, and I liked boots well-worn."

He continued saying, "When we were given the penalty, I told Andi he must take it. We had other options, men skilled at such shots, but Andi shared my quarters, and I knew he was the right man for the task."

Brehme, who as previously mentioned had netted a penalty with his left foot in the shootout victory over the Mexicans in the 1986 quarterfinals, did strike home the lone goal with his right to claim for Germany the trophy.

Brehme remains the sole player in the history of this grand quadrennial tournament to have scored goals from the mark with both his right and left feet.

Curiously, against Yugoslavia earlier in Italia '90, Matthaus did become the only player to ever score from outside the box in this grand tournament with both his right foot and his left.

Lothar is the most capped player of all time for Germany with 150 appearances and 23 goals. He is on the FIFA 100 list of the greatest living football players chosen by Pelé. Many say he is one of the best midfielders to ever play the game!

Lothar Matthaus

Champion's League Final. The Champion's League Final always draws a crowd. You might even come across newspaper ads reading,

"A handsome wealthy local man will marry you if you are a woman who has tickets to the Champions League final. Anyone who is interested in meeting must first send in a photo of the tickets."

Quiz question 3. What is the correct ball pressure for a ball?

A. Between 8.5-15.6 lbs./sq in.

B. Between 15.6-22.5 lbs./sq in.

C. Between 22.5-30.6 lbs./sq in

D. Any pressure so long as there is some pressure.

Answer or p. 98

Mad Dog Roy. Many had the opinion that Roy "Mad Dog" Keane was undoubtedly one of the most passionate people to ever lace up cleats for Manchester United. Few played with the fury of a man who some say could absolutely demolish someone's knees without losing a wink of sleep!

This Irish footballer won 19 major trophies in his career, and 17 of those were given during his time at Manchester United.

His resume of hard fouls was longer than a giraffe's neck. Eventually, the football authorities had seen enough of Mad Dog Roy's antics, slapping him with an eight-match vacation and a $155k fine - that's more than most people have made in a decade!

While Old Roy tried to leash the inner psycho later in his career, those battles with fellow hot-head Patrick Vieira could still get downright nasty. You didn't want to get in the middle of those two or you might lose a limb!

Let this be a warning to all - if you ever find yourself on the pitch with Mad Dog Roy, say your prayers and watch your knees!

Roy Keane

Did I hear that right? "I would have given my right arm to be a pianist."

   -- Sir Bobby Robson. One of the greatest manages in English football in history.

Speaking of passion, here's one super-tough lady! Hope Solo has never hesitated to openly share her thoughts and opinions. She freely expressed what was on her mind without reservation.

In addition to the intense passion she brings to the United States national team, Solo has found herself in problematic situations numerous times throughout her career. In 2007, she publicly criticized her superior for what she believed to be a misguided decision. Unexpectedly during the London Olympics, she directly targeted NBC's Brandi Chastain on Twitter, consistent with her bold nature.

She served as goalkeeper for the United States women's national soccer team from 2000 to 2016, helping the team achieve World Cup champion and two-time Olympic gold medalist status. These accomplishments speak for themselves, showing her exceptional ability.

Some experts consider her one of the top female goalkeepers in history. She currently holds the United States record for most career clean sheets, or shutouts.

This fearlessness, coupled with the nearly eerie resolve Solo exhibits, suggests that if one has the determination to be among the best, there should be no hesitation to freely share one's perspective and showcase one's full capabilities to the world.

In 2022 she had a dark time. A tragic incident occurred when she was found unconscious behind the wheel of a vehicle in a shopping center parking lot in March with her beloved 2-year-old twins in the car.

She entered a treatment program to battle her disease of alcoholism, received a suspended sentence of 24 months, and was fined $2,500. She acknowledged that she was blind to the problem and not strong enough to ask for help. She realized no one can face addiction without assistance and she will carry the consequences forever.

It's been said many times a hard fall means a high bounce if you're made of the right stuff and admitting you need help is certainly a first giant step for getting back to recovery and back on the road to a great life.

Hope Solo

Just throwing stones. A football hooligan was in court facing charges of disorderly conduct and assault. The arresting officer explained to the judge what had happened to lead to the arrest.

According to the officer, the accused had thrown something into the nearby river. When the judge asked exactly what object had been thrown, the officer replied "stones, sir."

The judge responded that simply throwing stones did not seem like an offense worthy of the charges.

However, the officer provided an important detail, saying "It was in this case, sir. Stones was the referee."

"The Chopper." Ronnie "The Chopper" Harris was quite the character back in the day. With a nickname that sounds more fitting for a serial killer than a footballer, you just knew this Chelsea legend meant business on the pitch. He was one of the best defenders ever in the sport.

Folks still talk about how he struck fear into the hearts of opponents - and sometimes even his own teammates! This man had no problem leaving his signature on someone if it meant winning the ball. Some would say he was more dangerous than a group of drunken football hooligans armed with rusty cleavers.

The highlight of his intimidation tactics had to be during that infamous 1970 FA Cup game against Leeds. Old Eddie Gray was having a whale of a time as playmaker until Chopper came in with his trademark two-footed slide tackle. Let's just say Eddie was only good for spectating the rest of the match!

And Chopper kept up the hijinks at Stamford Bridge for a whopping 19 years. You just knew that whenever he laced up his cleats, there was bound to be some fierce defending on the pitch. The man was committed if nothing else!

Emmanuel Eboue - a true comedian. During his time at Arsenal, Emmanuel became known for his comedy and zany antics both in the locker room and out in public. Sources say teammates would often find Eboue watching cartoons naked, claiming the shorts were "too constricting."

Eboue is something of a legend at Arsenal. Every player who has attempted to fill the role of team comedian is held up to Eboue's lofty standard of great fun behavior.

He's truly one of kind. During Ivory Coast's final World Cup game in 2010, things were looking great as they led North Korea 3-0. But then, the Korean coach called over his captain for an intense team chat. And that's when things got interesting!

Out of nowhere, Eboue decided he just had to be part of the conversation even though he didn't speak a single word of Korean! He nodded along like he understood Korean, and everything being said. What a hilarious mix-up! You can see it on YouTube - it's one of the most bizarre World Cup moments ever. [12]

Fast forward six years later, and Eboue spilled the beans on what really went down. He said "People will never forget that moment! When their coach called over the captain, I just had to insert myself. Even though I didn't understand a word!"

The Korean players thought it was absolutely hysterical too. They'd ask him to say things in Korean as a big joke. Lots of laughs for everyone!

But that's not even Eboue's most outrageous stunt! One time at Arsenal's Christmas party, he dressed up head to toe as a tiger and jumped out to scare everyone as they arrived! Even teammates like Adebayor were shocked. Eboue would roar like an actual tiger - talk about commitment to the bit! No wonder Adebayor said Eboue was funnier than most comedians.

Eboue was such fun that a popular chant amongst Arsenal fans when he took the pitch was "We've come to see the Eboue show!" And on certain days, crazier than a bag of cats, he was easily the most entertaining act on the field, whether he meant to be or not.

Emmanuel Eboue

Andoni "The Butcher of Bilbao" Goikoetxea.

Did you know that after almost ending Diego's career, Andoni proudly displayed the cleat he did it with! Like a hunting trophy!

That was a somber day on 24 September 1983. Andoni Goikoetxea's vicious foul on Diego Maradona would haunt him for the rest of his days.

In a league match at Camp Nou, he ruthlessly tackled the Argentine from behind, and players around them heard the sickening crunch of bone breaking piercing the air. Maradona would never forget the sound, likening it to wood splintering.

The young star crumpled to the ground, his season shattered by the brutal assault. After, the English press branded Goikoetxea the "Butcher of Bilbao," that dark label followed him like a shadow for his remaining years on the pitch, a permanent stain on his legacy.

If you haven't seen him injure Diego Maradona, check out the YouTube in the references. [13]

Quiz question 4. Which of the following pieces of equipment is not allowed for any player?

A. Pants

B. Tape on socks

C. A shirt without sleeves.

D. Facemask

E. Baseball cap

F. Hijab

Answer on p. 98

An incredible game! From one incredible finish to another, Charlton Athletics' 1957/58 clash against Huddersfield Town in the Football League Second Division will surely go down as the most remarkable match you will ever see and one that demands attention.

Played in December 1957, Charlton were reduced to 10 men after just 27 minutes when captain Derek Ulton had to be rushed to the hospital due to a dislocated shoulder. Substitutions weren't allowed back then, and almost immediately, Huddersfield jumped out to a 1-0 lead thanks to Les Massie.

Huddersfield continued building their lead with two goals from Alex Bain, one from Bill McGarry and one from Bob Ledger— holding a commanding 5-1 advantage over the home side with only 27 minutes left!

But then something truly incredible happened. Johnny Summers and Johnny "Buck" Ryan each lit the lamp for Charlton within two minutes to cut the deficit to 5-3. Summers then scored in the 73rd and 78th minutes—tying the game at five goals apiece before netting his fifth goal of the night in the 81st minute to give Charlton a 6-5 advantage!

There were only a few home fans left in the stands when their team was down 5-1 with 10 men, yet visiting Huddersfield somehow miraculously drew level again at six-all with just five minutes to play before a last-second header by Ryan gave Charlton an incredible 7-6 victory!

Being down 5-1 with 27 minutes to go and already a man down, Charlton had fought their way back to take the win in the most dramatic fashion imaginable — leaving then Huddersfield manager Bill Shankly absolutely speechless.

Just goes to show there's some truth in the old saying, "Never give up, for that is just the place and time that the tide will turn."

A Football Team's Lead Executive Punches Referee.

The big match was postponed across the land after the top dog from one squad took out his rage on the referee.

In a bizarre turn of events, Faruk "Mad Dog" Koca, president of the notorious Ankaragücü club, decided referee Halil Umut Meler had made one too many mistakes. It was like a scene straight from "Rambo" - old Farook lost his cool and charged onto the field, winding up for a massive overhand right that connected square with Halil's jaw.

Meler hit the deck seeing stars brighter than the Turkish flag. When the dust settled, poor Halil was left looking like a smashed grapefruit. Some say you could hear the "thwack" all the way to Istanbul!

Faruk was later arrested by the local constables. I guess some would say he was not the brightest bulb in the box after that doozy.

Now dubbed the "Night of Fisticuffs," the Turkish football world was sent into an uproar. While Faruk claims he was just standing up for his squad's honor after some iffy calls, he's been banned for eternity.

The league will try to get back into action, but that shiner on Halil's mug could take some time to clear up.

The cops had to fight through the angry mob to help the fallen referee limp back to the locker room. Since the ruckus, Faruk has resigned. He said he was sorry to Turkish refs, sports fans and the country - but sorry doesn't undo leaving Meler looking like an extra from a low budget alien flick! Apologies only go so far when you've risked someone's health.

Faruk also dabbled in politics, but after that donnybrook his political aspirations were kaputski as he was suspended league-wide after a leading club official of the team attacked a referee.

Quiz Question 5. Which of the following results in an indirect free kick (as opposed to a direct free kick)?

A. Tripping an opponent.

B. Deliberate hand ball (other than by the goalkeeper),

C. Throwing a shoe at the ball.

D. Dissent, offensive language or abusive or obscene gestures.

E. Grabbing and holding on to the hair of an opponent to slow the opponent down.

Answer on p. 98

Reflection. "Don't ever say to me 'you haven't done your best' as I've always done my best. Well, most of the time…when I felt like it."

-- **Alan Shearer.** Named by the Football Writers' Association as Player of the Year in 1994, he won the PFA Player of the Year award in 1995. In 1996, he came third in both Ballon d'Or and FIFA World Player of the Year awards. In 2004, he was named by Pelé in the FIFA 100 list of the world's greatest living players.

Alan Shearer

Take your pick. "I definitely want Brooklyn to be christened, but I don't know what religion yet. I'm still deciding between Christianity, Buddhism, and Jedi."

-- David Beckham.

Tricking mum. "Every time I went away, I tricked my mum and did that to play football. So, I'd say to her I'm going to school but actually I would be out in the parks or the streets playing football. I always loved it!"

-- Ronaldo.

Quiz Question 6. A tough one. Explain why did Brazil's Rinaldo Luis Nazario changed his hairstyle after Brazil beat England in the 2002 quarter finals? *Hint: to divert.*

Answer p. 98

Brave act. A man arrives at the pearly gates of heaven, where St. Pete is tossing the key up and down in his hands and sees the man approach. "So, happy to see you, sir, but before I can open these gates for your you have to tell me all the good stuff you did on Earth before I let you hang out with the angels."

The man scratches his head. "Uhh, to be really honest with you St. Peter, I didn't really do much good."

"Ah man," says St. Pete, "you at least do something crazy brave?"

"Wait, yes, yes I did!" says the man.

"Alright, alright, tell me about it," says St. Pete, leaning in with interest.

The man tells his tale. "I was reffing' the sickest game ever between Liverpool and Man U, zero to zero in the second half on the verge of OT. And I dropped the sickest penalty call, right against Liverpool in front of the Kop!"

St. Pete's eyes go wide. "No way! That's the definition of balls of steel! Just one thing though - when did this go down?"

The man smiles sheepishly. "About two minutes ago..."

Camus: Football Taught Him Morality and Obligations.

The sage doth say that from the beautiful game of football he hath derived all insight into virtue's demands and duties of mankind. *"Through the field of play where competition and cooperation find balance, nature's lessons shine through to guide one down wisdom's path. For it is there that order, teamwork and fairness teach us how to live with heart and soul. The noble sport instills empathy, discipline and fair play to build community among diverse peoples."*

Thus, from kicks and headers, this thinker learned life's deepest truths to enlighten others through works as immortal as the passions football doth inspire.

Dad football joke. Q. Where do football players go to dance?

A. The futball!

Player Headbutts Own Teammate. The Colombian football scene was rocked by an all-out brawl between supposed teammates. This wasn't the one team brawling with the other team brawl. This was an intra team brawl.

During a crucial late-game free kick for Atletico Nacional, star strikers Dayro "El Toro" Moreno and Jeison "Cabeza Dura" Lucumi got into a heated dispute over who would take the shot.

Eyewitnesses report that Moreno was casually bouncing the ball like a basketball as he strolled up to put the team on his back, when Lucumi came barreling in with his head down like a bull seeing red. Lucumi lowered his dome and charged straight into Moreno's face and gave him a bone crunching.

Referees immediately flashed the red card as Lucumi began headbutting everything in his path, including the corner flag, a ball boy, and the stadium jumbotron.

Moreno, dazed from the brutal headbutt, stumbled around like a drunk until teammates restrained him from going after Lucumi with a flying knee.

After order was restored, Nacional had to finish the match with only 10 men. The loss of scoring opportunities from the ejection was surely a factor in the 0-0 final score. Atletico's manager could only shake his head in disbelief at the locker room antics and reportedly said, "These guys need to get their heads checked, literally and figuratively."

It's clear there are still differences between Lucumi and Moreno. Fans can only hope they settle their differences in a sanctioned boxing match rather than further sullying the beautiful game with more head trauma on the pitch.

Origin of Women's football The Origin of Women's Football The British Ladies' Football Club, formed in 1895 in Great Britain, was one of the earliest women's association football teams. Lady Florence Dixie, an aristocrat from Dumfries, served as the patron for this pioneering team. Its inaugural captain was Nettie Honeyball, though her actual name was likely Mary Hutson.

The club held its first public match on March 23, 1895, in Crouch End, London. The match featured teams representing the North and South regions of England. The North emerged victorious with a score of 7-1 in front of an estimated audience of 11,000 spectators.

The British Ladies' Football Club and associated squads playing under different names regularly competed in matches until April 1897. The club also had a brief revival from 1902 to 1903 before disbanding again.

British Ladies' "North" team, pictured on 23 March 1895

Until the 19th century, women's participation in football was largely limited to folk rituals associated with marriage customs. For example, in Inverness, single women would annually play a match against married women while prospective husbands watched.

The first ever recorded women's football match took place on May 7, 1881, at Edinburgh's Hibernian Park. Billed as a Scotland-England international, two theater entrepreneurs organized it. Scotland won 3-0.

On May 16 of the same year, the teams played in Glasgow in front of over 5,000 people. However, the match was abandoned after a violent pitch invasion where the women players were "roughly jostled" and chased as they left the grounds.

Further matches resulted in similar pitch invasions, ultimately ending this early attempt to introduce women's football.

The 1881 teams had no known connection to the 1895 British teams. It is uncertain based on media coverage at the time what exactly the pitch invasions were protesting. However, the tone of press coverage, which would dominate how women's football was portrayed for the next century, clearly established in 1881 a barely disguised contempt regarding the players' appearance, costumes, and quality of play, coupled with the prevailing view that football was a rough sport unsuitable for women.

Maybe? "All that remains is for a few dots and commas to be crossed. And maybe a few T's to be dotted too?"

‒‒ **Mitchell Thomas.** He was a former English footballer and played as a defender and was fairly successful and well paid. He was a starter when he played for Tottenham Hotspur in the 1987 FA Cup Final.

That old black magic. It seems the stars of Africa just can't get enough of witch doctors! According to former Republic of Côte d'Ivoire player Gilles Yapi Yapo, he was led down an insane path of sacrifice and debt to the tune of $200,000 by a traditional healer. He said the witch doctor put a spell on him and really messed with his head.

Yapi Yapo was going through some rough times with his old club Nantes when his uncle, in a moment of madness, suggested a visit to a Parisian potion slinger. Yapi Yapo reported that witch doctors enjoy a high status in the Republic of Côte d'Ivoire. But this shaman had some doozy demands like sacrificing chickens, goats and, of course, cold hard cash to undo supposed "curses".

When the witch doctor tried to get him to sacrifice his own kid, Yapi Yapo knew it was time to scram. After two years and $200 grand lighter, our guy was officially done being voodoo's victim.

Another Ivorian import, Cisse Baratte, also got hooked by hoodoo back in his football days. He started with magic potion showers and sacrifices, wearing a do-rag with Koran verses sewn in for luck. Dressing rooms were filled with players wearing perfumes and talismans from Senegal and Cameroon.

The recent brouhaha around French star Paul Pogba proved witchery in football is still going strong. Pogba's own brother and friend claimed he paid a witch doctor to hex teammate Kylian Mbappe!

Pogba and the hoodoo man denied the doozy deal, but it tends to show even the best players in the world can't resist having a little hexing on the other guys as long as it helps their game.

Favourite position. What is a ghost's favourite position when playing football?

A. Ghoulkeeper!

The country with the most fans! China has the most fans, but the strange thing is it has one of the worst records.

There are over 100 million Chinese people who love football. Their men's national team known as "The Dragon's Team" only made it to the World Cup one time back in 2002, and then lost all three games they played in the group stage.

Bloomberg reported on a TV documentary that came out recently with all the details about corruption scandal in Chinese football, the biggest thing in over 10 years and involved game fixing. [14]

China loves football and has over a billion people. Their leader, Xi Jinping, is a huge fan and is cleaning house. Since late 2022, Communist Party inspectors have arrested some well-known names in Chinese football who were accused of taking bribes, manipulating games, trading favors, etc.

The Chinese national team in a 2018 FIFA World Cup qualification match against Iran

One of the smallest countries. Bermuda has an area of approximately 54 square km. Their team is called the "Gombey Warriors." Along with cricket, football is one of the most popular sports.

In 2019, Bermuda made their debut in the CONCACAF Nations League. In League A, Bermuda were placed with Mexico and Panama but finished at the bottom on goal difference, so they had to play in a Gold Cup qualifying round.

Bermuda beat Barbados 8-1 in the first qualifying round but then lost to Haiti 4-1 in the final round, so they got eliminated.

It's best to think you're not the best. Mia Hamm, a former professional football player and two-time Olympic gold medalist.

Mia has humbly said that while many consider her the best women's football player in the world, she does not think so. She believes that by maintaining the mindset of not believing the praise of others, it helps to push her to achieve more and potentially earn that title someday.

She has said many times that "those who say winning is not everything have likely never won anything before." She is only implying that competitors strive to win and seeing success as the primary goal.

And she teaches other players to be aware that if a team is able to intimidate you physically and gain the upper hand in that way, they have essentially already won. She deems it necessary to have mental toughness and not let opponents gain an edge through intimidation tactics.

She only views herself as part of a team rather than an individual competitor. She works to support her team, defer to team strategies, and make sacrifices that benefit the team overall. Hamm believes that the team as a whole, not any single player, should be considered the true champion.

Mia Hamm's competitive mindset during her successful career has made her one of the world's best women's football players.

-- **Mia Hamm**. Besides two Olympic gold medals, she was a two-time FIFA Women's World Cup champion. She spearheaded the Women's United Soccer Association, which was the first professional women's soccer league in the United States.

Mia Hamm

Top Three most viewed sports events in the world.
The most viewed sporting events in the world never cease to amaze with their jaw-dropping viewership numbers. Some of these top 10 sports events might surprise you with just how many eyeballs they attract, and some may not.

- Kicking things off at number one is the event of events -- the FIFA World Cup of Football. With a staggering 5 billion viewers, you better believe the entire globe comes to a screeching halt every four years to watch international football supremacy be decided.

  The competition and drama is simply unmatched. The next World cup returns to North America for the 2026 World Cup hosted by Canada, Mexico and the United States.

- In at number two is the grueling Tour de France cycling race with an incredible 3 billion viewers glued to their screens. I am constantly in awe of the sheer physical and mental strength these athletes display as they pedal hundreds of miles over multiple stages. The 2024 Tour de France promises to be just as epic.

- Coming in third is the Cricket World Cup attracting a massive 2 billion viewers. As I'm more of a baseball fan, I have to admit my surprise at seeing cricket on this list! But with 10 teams competing in it over six exhilarating weeks, it's no wonder the Cricket World Cup is such a global phenomenon. It truly is a sporting extravaganza!

No yellow card for me! A player was just about to be given a yellow card for punching another player in the face, but then the ref noticed the player was an amputee. No 'arm, no foul!

Going out in style. It was a bittersweet day on October 1st, 1977, as football legend Pele played his final match. The friendly exhibition between his former clubs, New York Cosmos and Santos, held much more significance than a typical friendly.

Though Pele originally hailed from Brazil, he had found a home across the ocean in America after being persuaded by the Secretary of Foreign Affairs to bring his talents stateside and grow the beautiful game in the United States. He joined the Cosmos in 1975 and immediately became a superstar.

By the time of his retirement, Pele was viewed by many as nearly divine for his accomplishments on the pitch. Even the great Muhammad Ali, one of the most iconic athletes of all time, made the trip to witness Pele's swan song.

The match began with Pele wearing the green and white of Santos, and he delighted fans with a vintage goal for his boyhood club. At halftime, he emotionally switched kits to don the blue of the Cosmos, capping his time in America.

As the final whistle blew, ending Pele's incomparable career, tears flowed freely from all in attendance. His fellow players wept as they embraced their legend of a teammate, while supporters sobbed at the realization, they'd never again see Pele perform his magic on the field.

The next day, newspapers reported the heavy rain that fell from the sky during the second half. "Even the sky was crying" one headline poetically declared. Truly, it was impossible for anyone present, or anyone who loved the beautiful game of football, not to feel deep sorrow at having to say goodbye to the greatest of all time. Pele's farewell match was a heartwarming yet heartbreaking celebration of a player who transcended sports.

Edson Arantes do Nascimento (Pele)

Watching the game. Jerry was relaxing at Bransbury Park watching the men play when all of a sudden, he spots the ref make a call that had him seeing red.

He shouts out, ""Hey ref you might want to check your voice mail YOU'VE MISSED A FEW CALLS!"

As play continued, he shouted out more, "Hey ref! What game are you watching?!" And "How much are they paying you?"

He continued, "Hey ref! I've got one word for you! SPECSAVERS!"

Well, the ref had finally had enough of Jerry's mouthing off. He storms over, gets right in Jerry's grill and yells, "I'll have you know I've been watching you heckle for the past 20 minutes pal!"

Jerry replies without missing a beat "No kiddin'? I thought for sure you were too busy watching the game!"

The Legend of Geoff Hurst and the Phantom Goal of 1966. It was the climactic moment that defined a nation - Geoff Hurst, with England clinging to a one goal lead in extra time of the 1966 World Cup Final, unleashed a ferocious right-footed strike that crashed into the underside of the crossbar.

As the ball ricocheted straight down, bouncing and bobbing along the goal line like an unsteady rollercoaster, Hurst and all of England held their breath. Would this shot be the one to secure football immortality? Or would fate steal glory at the very last moment?

To this day, no one knows for certain if the entirety of the ball crossed the line before being cleared, but in a moment that will echo through history, the goal was given.

Hurst wasn't done yet - he would complete his iconic hat trick to cement England as champions, the only man to ever score three in a World Cup final.

But it is that second goal, the one shrouded in mystery, that cemented Geoff Hurst as a legend and defined the drama and controversy that can emerge in football's greatest showcase - the 1966 World Cup Final.

Hurst's trading card from the Mexico 70 series issued by Panini.

It happened so quickly! The 1986 World Cup quarterfinal match between Argentina and England had one of the strangest acts of unfairness in football history. Diego Maradona, Argentina's star player, according to most opinions apparently punched the ball into the net with his fist. It was infamously called "The Hand of God." [15]

Yet the referee was either distracted or just simply missed it, refusing to acknowledge the blatant handball that everyone else saw as clear as day. In any event, Maradona and his teammates celebrated shamelessly, glorying in the goal!

While Maradona later scored a more legitimate goal, his apparently dishonest first strike tainted the entire match. Argentina's victory meant a place in the semifinals, but it became a stain on the game.

The Epic Battle of Lusail Stadium! The legendary showdown between the Netherlands and Argentina in the 2022 FIFA World Cup quarterfinals will be remembered as one of the most amazing and intense football matches in history!

Dubbed "The Battle of Lusail", this epic clash took place under the lights at Lusail Stadium in Qatar on December 9, 2022.

It was a clash for the ages between these two fierce footballing rivals. The Netherlands and Argentina had faced off nine times before, with victories seesawing back and forth between the two. Their last meeting, the dramatic 2014 World Cup semifinal that Argentina won on penalties, added fuel to the fire.

This matchup was hyped up to be the most incredible of the tournament. The Dutch entered on an incredible 19-match unbeaten streak. But their manager Louis van Gaal's comments about Argentine captain Lionel Messi seemed to light a powder keg! Van Gaal stated the usually elusive Messi left opportunities if pressure was applied, and that the Dutch had a "score to settle" from 2014.

The intensity and drama lived up to the billing. Spanish referee Antonio Mateu Lahoz issued card after card for a Guinness World Record that still stands today with a record 18 yellow cards and even one red, showing how passionately these two clashed.

The stage was set for high drama in this shootout. Van Dijk strode up, nerves of steel, to take the first penalty for the Oranje. But his shot was thwarted by a dazzling save from Argentina's daring goalkeeper, Emiliano Martínez.

Now Messi took center stage, calmly slotting his penalty past the keeper to draw first blood for La Albiceleste.

Martínez was in his element, employing every trick and tactic to unnerve the Dutch takers. Prior to Berghuis, he toyed with him, feigning to hand over the ball, before another stop from Martinez.

Paredes found the net to double Argentina's lead. Then as Koopmeiners prepared to shoot, Martínez kicked the ball away in a display of gamesmanship. But Koopmeiners kept his nerve, pulling one back for the Netherlands. Gonzalo Montiel answered for Argentina, restoring the two-goal advantage.

Weghorst dragged the Dutch closer with his strike. He confronted Fernandez after words were clearly exchanged. But Fernandez wavered, sending his shot wide to keep the score at 3-2. De Jong dispatched his penalty, despite Martinez' antics, to level things up at 3-3.

All eyes turned to Lautaro Martinez for the decisive moment. As he walked up, the Dutch players swarmed, looking to rattle him. But Dumfries' yellow card challenge only steeled his resolve. Martinez found the net, securing victory for Argentina in the most dramatic of fashions.

Argentina's World Cup journey would continue, while the other's dreams were dashed. This epic "Battle of Lusail" instantly became one of the most amazing and memorable matches in World Cup history!

The pig who loves football. My pet pig loves football. Usually, he plays clean but as soon as he's in mud he's Messi.

5 Hilarious Reasons to Become a Football Referee.

First reason. Football rules confuse you more than the instructions for your new wireless printer. Become a ref and you'll be the most clueless person on the field!

Second. While others head indoors to escape awful weather, you live for frolicking freely in the elements. Frostbite and hypothermia have never sounded so fun!

Third. Instead of drowning out hecklers, you feed off their fury like fine wine. The nastier they cuss, the more your day is made.

Fourth. Indecision is your superpower. Whatever call you make will surely be wrong.

Fifth. Nothing says "living the dream" like stripping down in cattle sheds between cows and cowpies. The refs' locker room -- where ambience comes to die.

Mega Football Coaching Bash Breaks World Record.
It's great to get lessons and improve your ability. Ever take a group lesson? Well, if you are a coach and are interested in World Records, the largest football lesson had a record 956 participants. This was achieved by the San Jose

Earthquakes (USA) in Morgan Hill, California, USA, on 3 June 2023. San Jose finally made it into the record books!

The San Jose Earthquakes hosted this event and held a massive lesson on dribbling, passing and shooting drills led by retired pro Shea "Skills" Salinas.

For 30 minutes, the field was filled with football fans and future stars learning the fundamentals. But this was no ordinary practice - it was a record-breaking attempt! And with over 900 athletes in attendance, the Earthquakes now hold the title for Largest Football Lesson.

After working up a sweat in the sun, all the participants cooled off with a free drink and commemorative t-shirt. It was the perfect way for the community to come together, have fun and make history as a team. Extra special for the local youth teams to learn from a pro too.

A huge congratulations to the Earthquakes for organizing such an epic event. The energy was off the charts as players of all ages joined in the action. The previous record was left in the dust, and football dreams were ignited for years to come. This was one record-breaking party no one will forget!

1994 FIFA World Cup - A very sad story.

Andres Escobar was murdered because of his own goal at the 1994 World Cup. [16] It occurred in Colombia's second group match against the hosts USA. Stretching to block a cross from USA's midfielder John Harkes, he inadvertently deflected the ball into his own net, sealing his tragic fate. The United States took a 1–0 lead and ended up winning 2–1.

Five days after Columbia's elimination from the 1994 FIFA World Cup, Andres decided to return to Colombia. When he arrived back, he contacted a few friends, and they went to a bar in the El Poblado neighborhood in Medellín. Coming out of the bar, they went to a liquor store, then went to the El Indio nightclub. [17]

He split up from his friends and about 3 am the next morning, he was by himself in the parking lot of the El Indio nightclub sitting in his car, when three men appeared.

An argument ensued and two of the men took out handguns. Andres was shot six times by one of them. The shooter shouted out "Goal!" (in Spanish) after each shot -- once for each time a football announcer had said it during the broadcast. [18] They drove away in a pick-up truck, leaving Andres to die.

Andres was taken to a hospital but died 45 minutes after his arrival at the hospital.

The BBC issued a public apology after a BBC football pundit made a bad off the cuff remark during the World Cup's Round of 16 match between Argentina and Romania showing disrespect for the Argentine defender. [19]

More than 120,000 mourners attended Andres' funeral.

Every year people honor Escobar by bringing photographs of him to matches. In July 2002, the city of Medellín unveiled a statue in honor of his tragic memory.

A man was arrested a day after the shooting. He confessed to killing Andres and convicted and sentenced for the horrendous crime. [20]

More sad stories. Emotions run high in South America when it comes to football. After devastating losses, riots are commonplace, as are dark acts between opposing supporters (and the plague of hooliganism). But when the focus shifts to the referee, things can take a sinister turn.

In 2013, a Brazilian referee battled with a player and stabbed the player on the pitch. Friends and relatives of the wounded player stormed the field, stoned the referee to death, dismembered him, and placed his head at the center circle as a grim reminder.

Tragically, the violence continued. In another instance, an Argentine referee, César Flores, issued a red card to a player for reasons still unclear. The man left angry, retrieved a weapon from his things, and returned looking to confront the official.

He fired three shots, one each at the head, neck and chest, and the 48-year-old died from his wounds. [21] Another player was also struck but survived.

While many parts of Europe, especially England, have made strides against hooliganism and violence in the field, South America has a long road ahead. The looming threat of such barbarism and loss of life makes one Brazilian referee's choice to carry a weapon seem a bit more understandable, though still disturbing.

Rinaldo's mindset.
Rinaldo has often said he loves things done well and constantly pushes himself with an endless desire to learn, improve and develop his abilities to the highest level. He is the only male player to score a goal in 5 different World Cups. And he's always striving for excellence and motivating himself to new heights!

Many renowned psychologists suggest the best ways to motivate yourself or coach others to reach their absolute full potential when they are on the pitch is to set clear and exciting goals that can help players focus their efforts and stay motivated.

Many feel that players should break down their goals into smaller, achievable steps to make progress and celebrate every win along the way.

Visualization can be a strong tool to increase motivation when they vividly imagine themselves performing amazingly well on the field, scoring incredible goals, and winning games. It helps players build sky-high confidence and stay motivated to achieve their goals.

Watching game highlights of the best stars or reading electrifying stories about their success also helps to keep motivation and keeping players positive.

Getting support from coaches, trainers, family, managers, teammates or anyone can help keep the motivation going. Players should seek constructive positive feedback to help them improve.

Staying Positive: Players should focus on their strengths, celebrate their successes like they just won the World Cup, and learn from their mistakes. They can also use enthusiastic self-talk to overcome negative thoughts and stay motivated towards their goals.

Many say Rinaldo has a burning desire for success and his record certainly speaks for itself. At the center of Cristiano Ronaldo is a strong work ethic. He trains at the gym with relentless training routines and understands that hard work is the master key to unlocking his full awesome potential.

He keeps himself dedicated, disciplined and confident he will continue to improve. He has said many times, "love of the sport makes him strong, and another's hate or jealously makes him unstoppable."

This looks like a good spot! Why doesn't Pakistan have an international football team? Because each time they get a corner, they open a shop.

Quiz question 7. Which former FIFA World Player of the Year became President of his home country in 2018?

Answer on p. 99

The FIFA Fan Festival™ The FIFA Fan Festival is one of the greatest places to visit during Men's and Women's FIFA World Cup matches! It has the most amazing World Cup atmosphere where you can cheer on your favorite teams while also enjoying an insanely fun football and entertainment program.

You'll see the greatest football alongside awesome music, local culture, and lifestyle - it truly is the ultimate football party and celebration!

This festival is an official site for all FIFA events and the central location where fans from around the globe come together to share their passion and excitement for football. You'll feel the unique energy of the World Cup like nowhere else!

The FIFA Fan Festival is a core part of experiencing the World Cup spirit in each host country and city. Whether you're a die-hard football nerd, casual fan, or just love music, food and culture - this festival gives everyone an incredible way to bond over the beautiful game in the most festive setting. You don't want to miss out on the non-stop excitement!

Best place to buy a shirt. What is the best place in the United States to buy a new football shirt?

A. New Jersey

I don't pose in my underwear. "Hey so I'm just not into posing in my underwear. Red carpets really aren't my thing. Give me the nice green grass any day.

"And another thing, after the games all anyone ever talks about are the goals, chances, and assists. But people tend to forget that as the goalkeeper, I'm out here making tough saves and really putting my body on the line. Not to mention I'm starting a lot of our plays with how I distribute the ball. So don't sleep on what I do out there!"

-- **Manuel Neuer** is an amazing professional footballer and has been a prominent goalkeeper for Germany. He represented both his national team and his club team, Bayern Munich, where he serves as captain.

Neuer is considered to be one of the greatest goalkeepers in the history of the sport. His unique playing style has earned him the moniker of "sweeper-keeper" as he is known for rushing aggressively off his goal line to anticipate opposing players, even venturing outside the penalty area at times. The International Federation of Football History & Statistics recognized his excellence, naming him the best goalkeeper of the 2011-2020 decade.

Neuer holds several impressive records for his position. He has recorded more clean sheets than any other goalkeeper at 223. He also has a record of 21 clean sheets in a single season. Reaching 100 clean sheets faster than anyone else, Neuer accomplished this milestone in just 183 games. Remarkably, as the only goalkeeper in the German Bundesliga to make over 100 appearances, Neuer has conceded fewer goals than the number of matches played. [22]

Manuel Neuer

Smart kids. Why do kids who play football do so well in school?

A. Because they use their heads.

Referee's quick thinking and admirable teamwork. When Denmark's star midfielder Christian Eriksen shockingly collapsed in the middle of their Euro 2020 opener against Finland, referee Anthony Taylor sprang into action immediately, waving the medics onto the pitch with urgency.

Anthony reported he knew something was terribly wrong right away because of the look on Christian's face and how he dropped to the ground.

Since the referee's response was so quick, the emergency medical team was able to immediately perform life-saving CPR on Eriksen, who suffered cardiac arrest and they also used a defibrillator to revive him. A doctor later reported Christian would have been a goner otherwise.

Simon Kjaer, captain of the Denmark team and friend of Christian also was among those who jumped into action. Within seconds, Kjaer rolled Eriksen onto his side to clear his airways and start the process of CPR. Kjaer then stepped aside for the medical team and went to console Eriksen's partner on the sideline.

The rest of the Denmark's team formed a barrier around Eriksen while he received treatment for privacy and better convenience for the medical team to work on him.

As the teams awaited word on whether to continue the match, Finland supporters started chanting passionately, "Christian! Christian!" The Danish fans roared back shouting eagerly, "Eriksen! Eriksen!"

What could have been a nightmare ultimately transformed into a story of quick thinking, bravery, insight and teamwork.

Referee Anthoy Taylor

How Football Brings the World Together.

Football has a way of bringing people together from all walks of life. Whether you're on the field or in the stands, the game transcends differences and unites us through a shared love and passion.

Out on the pitch, teammates bond over perfect passes and goals. In the stands, strangers become friends, celebrating the wins and supporting each other through the losses. The game fosters a great community wherever fans gather.

Football speaks a language all its own, one we all understand. It doesn't matter where you're from. When supporters meet, any prejudices melt away in the joy of the beautiful game. New friendships form across cultural lines.

Major tournaments like the World Cup are a reminder of football's power to inspire. For a few special weeks, over a billion fans worldwide join as one family. Communication is enhanced and barriers fade as we cheer and commiserate as one.

When the final whistle blows, the emotions feel universal. We may bleed different colors, but our love for this game runs deep. It's a reminder that however small, football has the strength to bring people together and show our shared humanity. This is its greatest victory.

When the final whistle blows, tears and cheers erupt as one. Win or lose, your heart overflows with the knowledge that, for a fleeting moment, you were all part of something spectacular. Something bigger than the game itself.

This is the power of football - to transcend who we are and see who we can become. This is why you love this game. Why we all do.

"Some people think football is a matter of life and death. I assure you, it's much more serious than that."

-- Bill Shankly.

_____ ♠♠ _____

Answers to Quiz Questions

1. A. True. The rules on a free kick provide that it can be taken by lifting the ball with a foot or both feet simultaneously. Law 13.2.

2. D. The pitch of the field can be anywhere from 100-130 yards long and 50-100 yards wide, grass or artificial turf, but the field has to be green (or as close as possible).

3. A. The ball must be 0.6 to 1.1 atmosphere at sea level, with a circumference of 27-28 inches. And that is Between 8.5-15.6 lbs./sq in.

4. C. A shirt without sleeves. Jerseys must have sleeves, whether long or short.

5. D. Dissent, offensive language or abusive or obscene gestures. The other infractions result in a direct free kick.

6. Answer: It was in the sweltering summer of 2002 that the legendary striker known as Ronaldo Nazario found himself in a moment of crisis. As the World Cup raged across the lands of Korea and Japan, Ronaldo's injury had become the talk of all spectators. His gimp leg had forced him from the quarterfinal match against England, though valiant Brazil did achieve victory that day.

Tired of the endless speculation about whether he could continue, the striker took matters into his own hands. Seeking to shift focus from his injured state, Ronaldo took scissors and carefully trimmed his locks. Leaving only a solitary patch near the crown, he emerged with a style unlike any seen before. His teammates laughed at the strange new 'do, calling it hideous.

9But Ronaldo did care about fashion - only that tongues might wag about something new.

His plan worked to perfection. When next Brazil took the field against the Turks in the semifinal, Ronaldo's leg held, and he found the net. Progressing to the final, he silenced the doubters through guile and goals. Though short lived, the curious hair became all the rage before Ronaldo bid it farewell. He took care also to apologize to mothers for the sons who mimicked his memorable mark. Through will and wit, Ronaldo overcame to bring glory to Brazil once more.

Ronaldo Luís Nazário

7. George Weah was the 25th President of Liberia (2018 to 2024). A legendary striker, he was no ordinary man.

Throughout his astonishing 18-year career scoring goals at world's biggest clubs, he showed the world that nothing was impossible. Like an eagle soaring through the skies, Arsène Wenger spotted his talent and brought him to fly in Europe with Monaco in 1988.

Weah's skills knew no bounds as he dazzled fans in France, Italy, and England while representing his homeland of Liberia on the international stage over 75 times. The striker's talent was undeniable as he won trophies with Monaco and Chelsea, while also shining for Manchester City later in his career. Always playing with the pride of his nation, Weah scored 18 goals for Liberia including appearances at two African Cups of Nations.

Even in retirement, Weah's greatness remains unmatched. In 2004, he was named the "FIFA World Player of the Year" and he was named in Pelé's list of the world's greatest living players, cementing his place among the all-time African legends. Weah's story inspired millions showing the world that with hard work and determination, all dreams are possible.

—— ✿✿ ——

Index

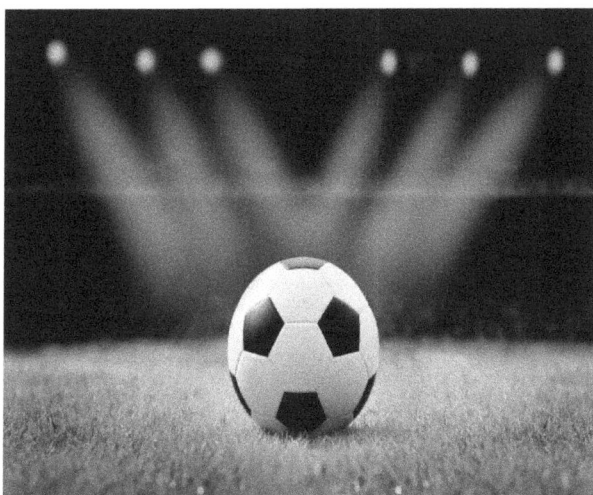

We hope you enjoyed the book!

Thank you for reading! If you liked the book, we would sincerely appreciate your taking a few moments to leave a brief review.

Thank you again very much!

Bruce Miller and Team Golfwell

Thank You

About the authors.

Bruce Miller. Lawyer, businessman, world traveler, private pilot, and award-winning author of over 50 books, a few being bestsellers, spends his days writing, studying, and constantly learning of the astounding, unexpected, and amazing events happening in the world today while exploring the brighter side of life.

He's the author of the popular Psychic Mystery/Thriller "Beware the Ides of March: A Novel Based on Psychic Readings" which was awarded a 2023 NYC Big Book Distinguished Favorite.

He's a member of the Australian Golf Media Association, The New Zealand Society of Authors, and the Independent Book Publishers Association.

Team Golfwell also helped author this book and were founded by Bruce Miller, and they are bestselling authors and creators of the very popular 370,000+ member Facebook Group "Golf Jokes and Stories."

Their many books have sold thousands of copies including several #1 bestsellers in Golf Coaching, Sports humour, and other categories.

We Want to Hear from You!

"There usually is a way to do things better and there is opportunity when you find it." - *Thomas Edison*

We love to hear your thoughts and suggestions on anything and please feel free to contact me at bruce@teamgolfwell.com

Other Books by Bruce Miller

- *Beware the Ides of March: A Novel Based on Psychic Readings (Awarded Distinguished Favorite by the NYC Big Book Award 2023).*
- *The Book of Unusual Sports Knowledge.*
- *Guy Wilson Creating Golf Excellence: The Genesis of Lydia Ko & More Stars.*
- *For a Great Fisherman Who Has Everything: A Funny Book for Fishermen.*
- *For the Golfer Who Has Everything: A Funny Golf Book.*
- *For a Tennis Player Who Has Everything: A Funny Tennis Book.*
- *The Funniest Quotations to Brighten Every Day: Brilliant, Inspiring, and Hilarious Thoughts from Great Minds.*
- *For Bright Legal Minds Who Have It All.*
- *A Complete Guide For Golfers Over 50: Reach Your Full Playing Potential*

And many more…

References

[1] How Messi explained his incredible goal against Getafe, YouTube,
https://www.youtube.com/watch?v=gwoKBi3FHvo&t=14s

[2] Ibid.

[3] The curse of Bela Gutmann, Wikipedia,
https://en.wikipedia.org/wiki/B%C3%A9la_Guttmann#%22T he_curse_of_B%C3%A9la_Guttmann%22

[4] AS Adema 149–0 SO l'Emyrne, Wikipedia,
https://en.wikipedia.org/wiki/AS_Adema_149%E2%80%930 _SO_l%27Emyrne

[5] AS Adema 149–0 SO l'Emyrne. Wikipedia,
https://en.wikipedia.org/wiki/AS_Adema_149%E2%80%930 _SO_l%27Emyrne

[6] Plateau United FC, Wikipedia,
https://en.wikipedia.org/wiki/Plateau_United_F.C.

[7] Rivaldo's Comedy Dive in 2002, You Tube,
https://www.youtube.com/watch?v=HMHZusksnXk

[8] Mauricio Baldivieso, Wikipedia,
https://en.wikipedia.org/wiki/Mauricio_Baldivieso#

[9] Italy v West Germany, Wikipedia,
https://en.wikipedia.org/wiki/Italy_v_West_Germany_(1970_ FIFA_World_Cup)

[10] Italy 4-3 West Germany Extended Highlights 1970 FIFA World Cup, YouTube,
https://www.youtube.com/watch?v=DIxr3kQnYvk

[11] Guinness Book of World Records,
https://www.guinnessworldrecords.com/world-records/longest-marathon-playing-football-(soccer)

[12] Eboue Listening In, YouTube,
https://www.youtube.com/watch?v=6LFZJIm3mD0

[13] La lesión más aterradora de Diego Maradona: ¿lo quisieron quebrar? , YouTube, https://www.youtube.com/watch?v=N8_JYHtvTS8
[14] https:/ China Airs TV Confessions of Corruption by Football Officials in Documentary, Bloomberg.com, /www.bloomberg.com/news/articles/2024-01-10/china-airs-tv-confessions-of-corruption-by-football-officials-in-documentary
[15] The hand of God, Wikipedia, https://en.wikipedia.org/wiki/The_hand_of_God
[16] Andres Escobar, Wikipedia, https://en.wikipedia.org/wiki/Andr%C3%A9s_Escobar#Own_goal_incident_and_subsequent_murder
[17] Ibid.
[18] Ibid.
[19] Ibid.
[20] Ibid.
[21] International referee Cesar Flores shot dead after showing player red card in Argentina, Independent, https://www.independent.co.uk/sport/football/international/referee-cesar-flores-shot-dead-after-showing-player-red-card-in-argentina-a6876836.html
[22] "500 up: Neuer's record-breaking Bayern career in numbers". bundesliga.com. 10 January 2024. Retrieved 23 January 2024

Milton Keynes UK
Ingram Content Group UK Ltd.
UKHW041426141124
2855UKWH00034B/103